THE
DICTIONARY
SPEAKS

Nicholas Murray

The Melos Press

First published in 2023
by The Melos Press
38 Palewell Park
London SW14 8JG

melospress.blogspot.com

ACKNOWLEDGEMENTS and thanks to the editors of *Scintilla*, and
Sunken Island: an anthology of British Poetry (Bournbrook Press, 2022),
where some of these poems first appeared.

Cover illustration by John-Paul Washer

ISBN 978-1-7394897-2-4

Printed by
One Digital, Unit 7 Woodingdean Business Park, Brighton, BN2 6NX

CONTENTS

O   5
THE DICTIONARY SPEAKS   6
AS WYNDHAM LEWIS SAID   7
THE BIRDS AND US   8
ENVY   12
WRITE ABOUT WHAT YOU KNOW   13
ODYSSEY   14
GWIL   15
MOAT   16
BIRTH OF A NATURALIST   17
COASTAL   18
WHIMBLE   19
THE PIPE SMOKER   20
LIMINAL   21
THE DELEGATE   22
PITY   23
FOLLOWERS   25
THE PRIME MINISTER REGRETS   26
TWO SONGS OF LOVE   27

O

It's all circumference, a tensile wall,
fencing us in, fencing us out.

A Quattrocento Pope demanded proof
from aspirant artists of their skill.

Plucking a brush from leather bag,
dipping its point in pigment, *SO!*

the painter drew a perfect circle
rotondo come la O di Giotto

and everyone admired this mark
that signified nothing, a nought

which in a row spoke of great riches,
singly, the pocket's plucked emptiness.

The O of exclamation or dismay,
the ovoid lips mouthing in silence

astonishment, regret, *jouissance;*
an all-embracing, gapless, ring

that closed within itself
immensities of sound.

THE DICTIONARY SPEAKS

I am the volume of the *OED*
that Auden, at Kirchstetten, used,
plumped-up as cushion to enable
his belly to approach the table
on rather less unequal terms.

Mostly ignored, week in, week out,
My friends and I in well-drilled rank
Dice segments of the alphabet:
A-Bazouki, Cham-Creeky, Poise-Quelt.
We sag the better sort of shelf.

Words are the power in our arsenal.
They crunch and crackle in the mouth
like bitten nuts, cracked-open seed;
their taste and feel, the poets are agreed,
more vital than the things they Say.

Too bad that obsolescence bites:
words don't keep still, they shift,
gain meanings like a spread of rust
or slowly settling household dust
that coats at night all furniture that sleeps.

They sit up straight and bawl,
behave unreasonably, or coarsely shout;
then, softer than murmuration of a dove,
whisper the sequent syllables of love,
proud of these various tricks they play.

As Wyndham Lewis Said

To Joyce: Rouen's facade, its Gothic plenitude,
teeming with carved saints, redundant clutter,
offers praise of *quantity*, dissolves 'the solid shell'.

Jim strokes his chin, his pockets full of paper scraps
on which a conversation's scratched, a name, a note,
a tearing from the *Zeitung*, patchwork stuff.

'Percy, I like my urban clutter, a verbal mess
stirred round and ladled out: world as it is,
words freely spun, not curbed by dogmas of design.'

[Percy Wyndham Lewis, *Rude Assignment* (1950), Chapter X]

The Birds and Us

Sparrows

On the sunny terrace
of the Sunday *boulangerie,*
whose crop of crumbs
delights their day,
the sparrows chirp and hop
as if on hidden springs,
pretending not to see
the croissant flakes
that drop from us,
as we pretend their fall
was just an accident.

Pigeon

The fact that we let drop
torn fragments of a loaf

is not a sign of love: observe
those spikes set on the pediment,

the netting stretched to keep you out;
winged vermin, streaking brick with white.

So when I find you at my feet
in this city avenue, a lump

of filthy feathers by the kerb,
compassion's limited, no tears,

just something to dispose of,
fodder for the bin-bag heap.

The poor are not like us;
we see the outside of their lives

and there's a hardness
in the clatter of a coin.

Gull

Open your mouth and *squawk!*

That bald white head,
those wet dark eyes,
splayed yellow feet
and predatory beak

don't make us think
you value what is delicate,
no shades of grey persuade
that anything but *squawk!*

and grab and pounce
are motors of your day,
dictating where you land
to snatch just what you want.

Snow-white, you keep yourself
well-groomed and neat,
but when the stiff beak parts
and raucous cries leap out

I judge it's time to leave,
to find a quieter spot,
and your response is clear:
open your mouth and *squawk!*

Quail

The quail is heard not seen, the twitchers say,
shy caller from the cereal fields;
we spear its eggs with toothpick, gulp in one go.

But here, this morning in full view,
the red-legged partridge with its young:
a foaming file that bubbles through the gate,

like altar boys in crimson cassocks
on childhood's summer 'holy days',
their hands around a candlestick of wax-streaked brass;

the plodding hymns that moaned along the wind
in weather joyful carolling should hymn,
to praise the summer and its waking scents.

Nuthatch

I am the nuthatch, rat-a-tat-tat
Up in the ash tree, listen-to-that.

Blue is my back or could it be grey?
Who but a twitcher could truly say?

Picking in the crevice for an insect or two;
walking in a zig-zag far above you.

High in the treetop, rat-a-tat-tat,
beak like a gimlet, get-a-bit-of-that.

Nuts are my weakness, hazel or beech,
acorns as a side-dish, or a bit of each.

On a day of sunshine up in my tree,
echo of my rat-a-tat, one-two-three.

ENVY

Ah, he's the same age as me,
same origins, same place,
but there the resemblance ends,
his progress smooth through Oxford,
etcetera, etcetera: a hot knife
lightly held above the butter
to be spread on a warm loaf,
a silver spoon peeping shyly
from the pot of thick jam.
The delicate charm of the effortless
working its slow, strong magic.
I offer no resistance. I am charmed.

WRITE ABOUT WHAT YOU KNOW

But what if that tale is rebarbative,
plays too easily the card of pain?
I too am entitled to a sunlit valley
down which a great river cascades,
bringing broken trees, fallen sheep,
but flanked by luscious meadows
where one can find a seat to sketch
the contours of the far hills whose slopes
are bronzed with late bracken, glinting,
pulsing a sharp shock through the air
which says that this also is experience:
exalted, yet a hair's breadth from terror.

ODYSSEY

I had quite forgotten: it is about the sea.
The salt, dark, implacable.

I am reading, on a slow ferry of the Cyclades,
of the arrival endlessly deferred,

of the man tested beyond limit
who will, of course, exact vengeance

from the drunken, meat-eating oafs
sprawled on his marble patio.

But first the sea, its massive swell,
its way of holding him, exerting power

through the imperative of tides,
noxious and 'fish-infested' depths

where only the blunt-nosed dolphin
yields a touch of the picturesque.

GWIL

Three things I remember: in pubs you played a saw
with a fiddle bow, and had a non-speaking role
in *Boys from the Blackstuff* but most of all
I see you at your window facing the shore

finishing watercolours of the flat land,
north of us, where distended trees
bent by the strong sea breeze
edged the potato fields of SW Lancs.

In your high room facing the river
you must have captured a ship or two
but all I have to remind me of you
are these framed fields: memory's sliver.

MOAT

'Horticultural Contractor' on the van's side
we rode to what the locals called 'the looney-bin'.

Sliding our mowers down the gentle slope
of the protective moat, thick with summer grass,

they buzzed, restive dogs at a lead's end;
let down, hauled up, by lengths of rope.

And then an inmate's head appeared;
his hand tossed down an empty matchbox

with the plea that we would fill it for him
with a humming, scrambling bumble-bee.

BIRTH OF A NATURALIST

Under the Bramley's prodigal spread,
heavy with green globes, they hopped
out of a dense jungle of wet weed:
tiny leaping things that rose and dropped:

their wrinkled skins light and gleaming
as they flicked themselves out of that green
tangle in the suburban garden's corner,
under the tree in rain, the pond unseen

(behind a neighbour's fence we guessed)
where they would hatch from grey jelly
unlike the jam jars we brought home,
only to see each tadpole turn up its belly

and float to the top, horribly dead.
Better admire this show of leaping frogs,
tiny and glistening under the tree,
where a soft rot of stacked-up logs

became their home, freely chosen.
Intent on their own absorbing ends,
they learned quickly to ignore us,
their fussy but irrelevant friends.

COASTAL

Here at the cliff's edge,
look down at your peril
at the turmoil of waves
that break on rocks
where foam slithers
and the seabirds search
for crevices to nest.

There's a stiff wind
coming from the ocean
shaking the caravans
parked in their reservation,
forcing the blown walkers
to put hand to head
or watch a hat fly up.

We obey the weather,
leaning into the breeze
to gulp the cleanness
of salty air, cant
towards buffets
that beat our faces.
Lifting our spirits.

WHIMBLE

When Whimble wears his cloudy cap
then Radnor boys beware of that.
                           Traditional rhyme

Behind the dunes we ploughed the soft sand path,
then crossed a fence to trespass on the sloping floor
of fallen needles, scattered cones, dark military ranks
of resin-leaking pines that closed out light.

Later, we watched them, waited for confirming truth,
that tightening cones predicted rain,
trusted their powers as we might solving creams
or headache pills, prepared for disappointment.

This Radnor hill whose crown is mist today
more surely guarantees the coming rain,
sheeting slant, dripping from stone,
spray hissing out from tractor wheels,

dark stain of damp on cottage walls,
gutters like racing streams, a surfing leaf
riding the brook's surface, its banks braced
for the thrill of trespass on the village lane.

THE PIPE SMOKER

I went to Hay to pay some bills.
On the crest of the hill above Hay I met a tall woman
smoking a clay pipe and driving a black donkey.

Francis Kilvert

Tall, beanstick-thin, well-weathered,
black hair free-flowing on a morning in July,
sun after thunder lighting the hills.

Between her lips the long pipe,
its white arc fragile and tender;
white against black, the bared teeth

of the donkey, careful on stones,
coming out of Hay, its rump
a dirty carpet streaked with mud.

And the man of God whose fine gift
for seeing things lights the day
as sunshine after sudden rain.

LIMINAL

I walk to England for my supper.
Wales soundly sleeps behind me

as I cross the bridge,
torchless in moonlight.

The privilege of border country:
to swap one's favours randomly,

crossing and recrossing
the map's short broken lines

that mark this place from that.
Not as wheat from chaff

with the confident promise
of the good won from the bad

but merely noting as you walk
in what way we co-exist

across assumed disparities,
of attitude or tongue;

pausing by the dark turbulence
of the swift and rising river.

THE DELEGATE

Dark suited, he leaves Gare Cornavin,
hauling a small case into driving rain.
On Lac Leman the *jet d'eau* wavers

as he shivers across the bridge
towards a memorised address:
the small hotel where long keys

are tied to a heavy ball,
and the concierge smiles doubtfully
at the man with steamed lenses

who has come with his bullet points
to enlighten the conference hall
between breakfast and a light lunch.

What are your Issues? she asks at supper.
He replies in perfect French:
to win more than one meal a day.

PITY

Let pity greet us from Argos like a gentle wind!
Chorus of the fifty daughters of Danaus, *The Suppliants*, Aeschylus.

Listen to us, arrived from Egypt,
harried and hassled by our men:
Black sisters, facing rape, ripped
from our homeland, in small boats.

King of Argos you have power,
the right to judge our claim.
We admire your bright shower
of clever words, their ethical finesse,

but remember Zeus whose eye
is watching you, unassuaged
by lawyer-smartness: try
to see what truly matters here:

not scruple's surplus, pause
for endless yes-but argument;
forget cold, coded laws
and let your human heart dictate.

Do you consider that we'd sail
for days across a chancy sea
just for the fun of it? Don't fail
us now in our extreme condition.

Pity's the gift the lucky spend,
from wallets fat with folded notes;
it costs you little, royal friend,
we'll do the rest if you just grant

23

a little space, a plot of ground,
some unused hectare we can sow.
Turn your head and look around:
your granaries full, just let a little go.

FOLLOWERS

Harriet Humblebrag has ten thousand followers.
They drag behind her: as the dark, dripping rope
of a tethered barge on which a bicycle, a potted palm,
a runcible white fence, clutter the silent deck.

Or the column of lost souls waiting to cross
to the fiery permanence of Hell.
They are obedient; they take their punishment
with the good grace of those who cannot lift an arm

to break the blow that comes at them athwart.
O, let her lead them to a sweeter place
where the finest grasses grow, and bright streams
course down a slope livid with asphodel.

THE PRIME MINISTER REGRETS

That smoking gun,
warm in my hand,
and the scarlet pool
on the tiled floor;

the white shirt spattered
and the mute stillness
of the cold corpse
might seem to some a proof

(now that you mention it)
of culpable wrong-doing.
But context is important here
and all is not what it seems.

I had no idea that the raised gun
and the pulled trigger
might result in such a scene.
Believe me, sincerely.

Do not rush to judgement,
or call me an arrogant oaf
whose lease is too long extended
who lies, easily, as others breathe

until the truth seems a word
light as an autumn leaf
that falls in a bright spiral
of papery flight, prettily.

12 January 2022

Two Songs of Love

I
Finger seeks the scar's shy traces
feeling for love's secret places;

private stories in the dark
place their cryptogram or mark

written in the crafty codes
unofficial smugglers' roads

use to show deep sunken lanes
turned to streams by summer rains

guiding lovers in the night
who see most clearly without sight.

II
Strike the string and beat the drum;
here the gaudy players come.
Sunlight glints from shiny brass
as the bright musicians pass.

Someone steals a small white hand
while all eyes focus on the band.
They draw aside and find a space
where hands and eyes and limbs enlace.

Fiddlers saw and pipers blow
but lovers do not care to go
where crowds clap hands and drum their feet,
they choose the private and discreet.